Catching Your Breath

for Simon

with love
from

CHRISTINE WEBB

Christine

INDEPENDENT INNOVATIVE INTERNATIONAL

Published by Cinnamon Press
Meirion House, Glan yr afon, Tanygrisiau
Blaenau Ffestiniog, Gwynedd, LL41 3SU
www.cinnamonpress.com
The right of Christine Webb to be identified as author of this work
has been asserted by her in accordance with the Copyright,
Designs and Patent Act, 1988. Copyright © 2011 Christine Webb
ISBN: 978-1-907090-49-3

British Library Cataloguing in Publication Data. A CIP record for
this book can be obtained from the British Library.

Designed and typeset in Palatino by Cinnamon Press.
Cover from original artwork © Tristan Campbell used with kind
permission.
Cover design by Jan Fortune-Wood.

Printed in Norfolk by MPG Biddles Ltd.

Cinnamon Press is represented in the UK by Inpress Ltd
www.inpressbooks.co.uk and in Wales by the Welsh Books
Council www.cllc.org.uk.

Acknowledgements

Poems in this collection have previously appeared in *Poetry London*, *Mslexia*, *Smiths Knoll*, on the *Guardian* website and in Carol Ann Duffy's Poetry Corner in the *Daily Mirror*. The following five appeared in *Bedford Square 4* (John Murray, 2010): 'A Family Programme', 'After That Hour', 'Horace in Eternity', 'On the Beach at Aldeburgh' and 'Trackside'.

Contents

In memory of Jackie Clarke, 1938-2006

Catching Your Breath

After that Hour

After that hour of sleep, you woke, and made
a little sound, between a cough and sigh.
The breathless nights were over: unafraid
after that hour of sleep, you woke, and made
no gesture of distress, but simply laid
your hands in mine. It seemed easy to die
after that hour of sleep: you woke, and made
a little sound, between a cough and sigh.

Revisiting that hour, as every day
I do, I find you waking from your sleep.
You never speak, but always look away:
revisiting that hour, as every day
lengthens your absence, I pretend you'll stay,
look at me, answer. Else why should I keep
revisiting that hour, as every day
I do, to find you waking from your sleep?

Salt

'Pig were allus a big job. Throat
to cut, quarts of blood. Harry'd
got in the way of it, years back
– his dad had taught him all the tricks,
how to manage the feet, keep away
from the teeth: a pig can land you
a fair bite. Use your muscles
– shoving, rolling it over. Guts
that hot you'd hardly credit.
Singeing. Scouring. A dead weight.

'We'd pack the meat down, in big joints,
shift them to lie snug. You'd hear the salt
crunch as you pushed your first lot in –
a good bed under the meat – handfuls
pressed down. Every space right solid.
Your fingers go numb. Little grains
get under your nails, skin's as rough
as pig's hide. End of day, your lips
taste salt. You breathe salt. Everything stings.'

Was this, then, how it was? Her voice
edges down the years, filters
through the salt grains, creaks under
that steady compression, as the air's
squeezed out.

　　　　　　Then the bad winter.
Ground stone-hard from November.
Kitchen tap lagged for weeks.
Birds died in mid-air.

And the phlegm in Harry's chest hardened,
burned. He shivered under the crackling
roof, labouring as crust after crust
of snow thickened. She toiled to and fro
with water, slops – piss, blood, bile.
One morning, the sky sick with yellowish
cloud, he stopped between one breath and
a silence, as the next one didn't come.
The clock ticked on. A few flakes swayed
down, gathered into a dizzying curtain,
steadied. She watched him as he cooled
– alone now, and the hill-track blocked.

Weeks passed. She baked bread, sliced ham,
banked the fire, slept when she could
until someone – farmer, doctor – broke through
the drifts, stared as her dry voice
croaked to a stop; asked, gazing round,
'Where…?' She stared back. 'I salted 'un.'

This was the story we heard. It stops
there: the bulky stranger we'd met
by chance, on the edge of a morning
view – sunlight on hills, the tang
of heather – spilled out his tale, was gone.
We were young. It was a curiosity
we scarcely revisited. But now I wonder:
how did she manage it? Did she lug him
off the bed before he stiffened? or wait
until the stiffness passed? Salting a pig
has its traditions: Bradenham, Gloucester,
York. Not all of them use a man-sized
trough. A table, then? But heaving him

up – the weight! Packing him down – the pounds
and pounds of salt, to bury them, the limbs
she'd loved, the lips she'd kissed, the plains and hollows,
the tender parts: did she break off to retch
or weep?

I think of her – how her hands would keep
the memory of his body – as I feel again
the curve and weight of your head
empty of everything except its mass
needing both my hands to lift it
and settle it, face upward,
on your stained pillow.

Catching Your Breath

Perfect

When you say, we've had good times haven't we?
– if I hesitate, it's not to deny

hours we've watched a loch shake its cross-hatched
nets of light; moments you've nudged me round

to catch a terracotta's blue and lemon
glaze, flash-dot of red on a woodpecker;

nights we've breathed beside each other, curved
like commas – no, it's that perfect

tense arrests me: though the grammars say
it always signals connection with the present,

you've made it clear our present's not continuous
with those good times, or if it is, the simple

past must be accepted as just that –
simply past, and all its acts perfected.

Catching Your Breath

Quick

You pulled in one breath at the edge of the playground,
clamped books to your head in an inverted V

and as the cracked note of the bell faded
into rain sizzling on lump-seamed tarmac

your long legs ate up the yard, wind caught at
flying edges of your clothes, your hair,

whipped horizontal streaks to blur your glasses –
till taking the staffroom stairs two at a stride

you landed with twelve and a half of the fifteen minutes
for coffee, back-chat, another cigarette,

before swinging down the corridor to bring
thirty children to their feet with a glance

that said you knew their names and all about them.
I studied you. There was nothing you couldn't do.

Catching Your Breath

Skip Lane

Don't you think my husband's sweet, you said
as you drove me back to my digs on the Birmingham road

in the car with a floor so rust-pocked that the jack
broke through three times the morning you had the puncture

and I must have answered somehow, though I forget
now whether it was his beard made me distrust him

or that he listened to you play a Chopin prelude
for me, and said he'd counted thirteen mistakes

while not acknowledging the only one that mattered
– any more than we did in your car that evening

nor during six weeks of frosty starlight, shivering
in Skip Lane, not daring to touch each other,

hoping that one of us would break through the talk
of politics, God, depression, with a simple kiss.

Catching Your Breath

Cannock Chase

I'm trusting to your sense of direction,
because I'm useless, you said, as we set off

across toughened bracken, snatching trails of bramble,
clumps of silver birch, though since you laughed

I took no notice, gave myself to our talk,
watched light on your cheekbones, gripped your wide

palm in its leather glove as you waited to steady me
over a stile. So when we paused for breath

an hour later, with not a clue about where
to look for the turquoise Renault, corroding still more

in the late October dew, I saw that you'd meant it
and that among these replicating tremors

of leaf, knots of grass, bushes, shadows,
we were lost, though neither of us yet said so.

Catching Your Breath

Knowledge

That moment suspended in the dull room
above the streets of the January town

(a branch pecked on the window, but the curtains
shut out the garden of dead chrysanthemums)

– undressing for each other the first time
all I saw was lit up by your body,

its gold and ivory. Such knowledge to bring away,
to carry wrapped through the streets, past naked trees,

into the school where heating pipes clanked and gossiped,
where blackboards expressed decorous equations,

where at the corners of corridors we might breathe in
to pass each other, but did not speak or glance

in case the doorways should break into leaf,
in case the books we carried should burst into flame.

Horace in Winter

Snow stacked up on the hill.
Creak and glitter of woods
under their load. Rivers
locked in frost.

Break the ice: heap
logs high on your stove,
open a vintage Shiraz,
splash out!

Leave the rest to the gods:
when the winds stop raving,
lashing the sea, there'll be peace
for ash and pine-tree.

Forget about tomorrow.
Count each day as a bonus,
go for love and music
while you're young,

untouched by age, bitterness:
the fields and the city squares
are sweet with nightly whispers,
those meetings

 – the soft laugh of a girl
in an intimate corner,
her hands, her arms, yielding,
yes, willing.

Horace in Spring

Winter's gone, and the breeze licks your face.
Boats grind across the shingle,
cows bellow, the farmer's itching
to get outside. Frost's just a memory.

Dancing's everywhere. Bass booms
from windows and from cars. The gods
of love, feasting and travel
call for worship, celebration

while death, who doesn't give a toss,
rattles at the door of the doss-house
and the Kremlin. You're feeling lucky?
Life says don't bank on hope:

here's night already, crowding in –
the shadow-land, the fleshless kingdom
where you'll not be placing bets, or staring
at the soft bloom on a lad's skin

– yes, he's the one draws sparks from the others
and the girls will be on fire any minute.

Horace in Eternity

He's made, he says, a better monument
than brass: something that will outlive
the weathering elements – wind, rain,
centuries of processions

while the priest climbs the Capitol
in the crowded silence, the Vestals pacing
behind. He'll be read for ever, he says,
and everywhere

even in the unfashionable provinces.
He's cracked the code, liberated
crystalline Greek forms
into the new music

of this Italian peninsula, won the right
to the immortal crown: the Muses should
be proud of him. And it's true, blast him.
None of us can catch

him as he soars ahead: we stumble on
reaching out for that elusive word
that would translate us into felicity
if we could find it.

Catching Your Breath

Visitor

The starling must have tumbled in down the chimney
and was balancing on the wardrobe. Till it moved its head –

you told me next day – you thought what a stupid place
they've put that stuffed bird. It was your first visit.

My father at tea-time, carving the cold ham,
roared that libraries should censor their holdings:

he'd never read such filth. Book should be banned.
Our teacups – the best set – rang with assault,

defence of free speech. Your hands moved on the table –
knife, fork, plate – while you followed our faces

(my mother sighing: What must you think of us?)
and later watched my father gentle the cupped

bundle of feathers – Come on, old lad, old lad –
in his brown joiner's hands, launch it into the night.

Catching Your Breath

Picnic

We spent our luxury slowly: time, sunlight,
strawberries, the glisten of juice and sugar,

wind stroking the grasses all one way
to a shine, a spider trusting its body

down a thread, curved legs quivering. You tilted
your spoon. I touched your hand. Last July

we hardly knew each other's name, and now –
Look! – *now* was a ripple swelling on the horizon

that ran lopsided, panted up, to offer
the fat pink bundle of his balls and penis.

We turned our heads, disdainful. Sorry, he mouthed,
and ran on. How could he imagine…?

your eyes asked mine. We breathed out laughter, dipped
deeper into the berries, licked our lips.

Catching Your Breath

Critical

Still taken aback by happiness, we lodged
in a village where the stream ran down a stair

of scales, music of half-tones, quarter-tones
too close to separate. A mile below the fall,

the loch. A morning in the sun, with books.
Plunged in Middlemarch, I forgot the coffee flask

wedged deep in the shingle, chink of pebbles
as feet shifted, ripples' shlup-lup-shlup

until a phrase surfaced, shaking its meanings
over me: 'those critical first months

of a marriage'. I looked across, drank in
this no-longer-stranger whose breath rose

and fell beside me. You raised your head,
smiled. That naked smile. I stared back.

Catching Your Breath

Whiteladies

Now can you smell it? I said, as we stood by the sign
to the old priory. The scent hung in the hedge –

warm, rounded as cinnamon, piercing
but not lavender. The leaves were dark with midsummer.

Behind us, the engine ticked down. A grasshopper somewhere
scraped its legs. So what is it? you said.

I followed the thread to the pale horns of bent-back
petals, open lips breathing, hair-fine stamens

trembling with pollen; snatched down a tangle
to thrust towards you – you as cream and gold

as this honeysuckle: my sweet ignoramus!
We should have leapt the gate, startled the ghosts

of the contemplative nuns with our laughter and kisses
– but the priory field was rough and full of thistles.

Catching Your Breath

Blessing

October city-smells: coffee, warm bread,
old drains. Garrulous, a tattered pigeon,

she seized on us. Notre Dame – you have been there? –
nothing to this small church. See, see the carving

inside: how the penitent turns to Our Saviour,
her lips, her hair, stone flowing like water,

you would say, no? I was married here,
and my daughter. But she has gone away. I come

each morning – she tipped her head, eyed us – to pray
for blessing on this wicked world. It is wicked,

is it not? I think often of my daughter.
Much wickedness. I wish you health and happiness.

Long life. I bless you. She drifted away.
The city breathed out. You lit a cigarette.

Three Museum Pieces

1
A Puritan Watch

It rests, two halves of a gold
walnut-shell, split to show
the solid oval watch that *may
have been Cromwell's*

that Milton may have heard ticking
in a pause between sentences
the candles becoming a blur
the window a glimmer

during those serious discourses on
the tenure of kings and magistrates.
'I like its plainness –
needing no adornment but itself'

and the Secretary pockets
the phrase, conjures *tresses
down to the slender waist*:
there is nothing he can't use.

2
A Very Small Exhibition

Tobacco-papers
and gold-dust measures
don't hurt, but soon
it's neck-rings, shackles,

neatly inked plans
of decks fleshed close
as the zigzag skeleton
of a herring.

3
Fly

Noon on Crete. Baked earth. A girl
steps from the blaze into the dim

store, where the pots stand as tall
as her breast, wider than both arms

at full stretch. Leaning in, she dips
a jug, wrinkling the dark oil

which closes with a soft slap
on itself. She breathes resinous

fruit, licks a bead from the rim
and flaps at a green-enamelled

fly, back-handing it to zoom
under the lintel, away from the cool

*'pithoi, used for storage, dating from
late Minoan Crete, and bearing all*

*the marks of a sophisticated
culture. Front of case, a gold bee*

*or, possibly, fly: techniques of granulation
and filigree are sufficiently advanced*

*in the insect's oval wings and segmented
body'*   so that with a furious buzz

it star-bursts the glass, whirrs out and begins
zinging up and down *late Minoan Crete,*

hurtling into *Archaic Greece, Ancient Near East*, gallery after gallery,

to reach at last the *Hall of Living and Dying* where it glitters and whines

in a figure of eight around the cases
enacting its name at all the staring eyes.

A Family Programme

Under the eye of the camera
the male swallow flies up to the nest
his beak full of surprises.

His wire feet hook
for a moment on the edge, as he inspects
the hot squirming nestful –

organs pulsing behind the paper skin –
picks out one squeaker
and drops it on the barn floor.

These were not his young,
say the presenters, who yesterday pointed
to the *devotion of a single-mother*

barn-owl, to the *tenderness*
of an osprey's beak, tearing
bloody fragments for a chick. The swallow

repeats his sequence – four, five –
tugs out the last chick by its claw,
dumps it, as the female

swoops in. With a quick flutter
and jerk, he mounts her,
their shadows feathering the wall,

and both whirr away. *Now
he will build a new nest.* He weaves and moulds
shiny globs of mud. Soon the female

will swell, strain, lay his eggs.

Catching Your Breath

Hands

Long before we touched, I'd learnt by heart
the long bones of your fingers, their stretch and spring,

had watched them span octaves, leap for a note,
flick-flick a cigarette – the milled wheel, cupped flame:

no surprise, then, the steadiness of your loaded
brush, gloss slicked to follow an architrave,

your nursing a chosen screw to balance, bite
and twist clockwise home, its bright head flush.

Down the decades I tracked running needle, hammer,
up-loop of a dropped stitch, pencilled charts,

but never caught the knack: fingers like dancers
(and you danced, too) could not steer mine from cobbling,

mis-shaping what would take all your powers to rescue.
Strange, to think we made anything together.

Catching Your Breath

Karl der Grosse

I hope you realise, you said, my stomach's
churning. Whatever for? I said, as the new Renault

splashed its butter-yellow through storms of July
traffic in Aachen. Your hands on wheel

and gearstick tightened. It's easy, I said,
there's the Parkhaus, just past the lights. Buses

swayed, thrummed towards us. Wipers squeaked
on the windscreen. Turn left, I said. There. Turn.

(I didn't drive then.) The Dom, when we reached it,
was cool, marbled. I don't know why I'd insisted

on Charlemagne's tomb, or which of us found it.
Crowned Emperor in Rome, AD 800.

There, I said. We must go to Rome next.
You drew a deep breath. Not if I'm driving.

Catching Your Breath

Rome

Let's not pretend. I could choose to recall us,
heads tipped back on a Sistine Chapel bench,

angled to see Noah's flood, trees with their hair
horizontal in the storm; drinking tall beers

on the Appian Way; dodging the papal speech
to scramble on the Capitoline, inhale the pagan

scent of wisteria – 'this morn of Rome and May',
I quoted, and you laughed, said it was April;

and could forget how we lost ourselves the first morning,
argued in St Peter's about the IRA,

or had to stop for your pull on a cigarette
at inconvenient corners – but to excise these

moments is to make the flawed, breathing
body of our life a marble simulacrum.

Catching Your Breath

Negotiations

It depends, said the adviser, as you caught your breath
after three flights of stairs, what you mean by ethical.

No arms dealers, you said, no rain-forest loggers,
no regimes that routinely oppress women.

And socks for the army? she asked. As we left,
our feet on the steps making dull music,

I watched your polished shoes, your flexing ankles,
thought about socks, boots. Sand. Long bones.

That December, as markets rose, fell, beckoned,
we collided at a stand of gilt-trimmed crackers,

each with hat and motto. I put the box back:
Piece-workers, I said, slaving for a pittance.

In the crashing aisles our arguments hissed and glittered,
fencing with the feet of soldiers, the hands of women.

Catching Your Breath

Hinge

There is no hinge, just as there was no moment
when either of us said, or when I thought, even,

This is the one you won't survive. Your breath
seeps away, a soundless puncture at the heart

of your resilience: the walk at Kleine Scheidegg,
its cowbells and thin-stalked flowers, or across

the Galataseray Bridge towards a skyline of
domes and minarets – these become epic, heroic,

become perspectives in a marvelled-at distance.
As air runs out we check milestones: no more

days on foot in the city, spadework in the garden,
dark resonance of an alto solo

– until, you tell me, only at the crossing into sleep
are you running towards some high horizon.

On the Beach at Aldeburgh

i.m. Julia Casterton

It's an untidy heap, this coast –
shingle thrown at random, as if the tide's
too disorganised to do it properly.

And the litter! – a gull's cast feather,
empty razor-shells, some in halves,
no use to anyone, not even a hermit crab.

The water mucks about, some rollers
sleek and regular, a glossy procession
where every seventh wave tops the others

– but too often they jump the queue, skid
and overlap, tilting their panfuls
of foaming omelette at my feet.

The light's all anyhow, one minute
hard and flat as a bone, drying the gleam
from the pebbles; and the next, sneaking

round the stacks of clouds – where look! God's
fingers shimmer, point to the sea as it roars
and dances, and a flung stone skips

five times, and the rollers lift shrieking
children, and the gulls ride the air and water

– and maybe you've risen, too, somewhere.

Horace at Sea

Who's the boy – slim, fragrant
with after-shave, pressing himself against you
now, in some quiet spot? Who
will watch you putting up that golden

hair he's tumbled? He'll soon be cursing
you, and the gods, and the weather, all
treacherous: dark winds, whipping
the sea into a rage he's never seen.

You taste so sweet today, he trusts you:
you're always free, always welcoming,
he thinks – can't imagine
how quickly the wind shifts,

how many ships you've wrecked,
mine being one. Half-drowned, gasping,
I escaped, offered my streaming clothes
in thanks to the sea-god.

Fitzroy

Fastnet   Shannon   Rockall   Bailey:
the shipping areas ring out their names
as regular as teatime, tracking, predicting.

Listen. There's a new name. Listen for Fitzroy
as the *Beagle* creaks and judders, its onboard
naturalist, when not puking, absorbed

in skins, bones, sketches, the shared cabin
ticking and crawling with many-legged life,
stacked with parcels for the next, distant, port,

bristling with notebooks. Every Sunday –
sea a milky scum, a bruising chop –
Captain Fitzroy reads divine service,

scans his crew, scrubbed and attentive on deck,
his passenger, head bowed: bids them lay bare
their hearts before God. Think of Fitzroy

decades later, as he bares his throat
to the slice and whistle of the razor.
Hear his name toll: *South Fitzroy, North Fitzroy.*

Cocklers

Half dusk. Low water. A frieze
of figures stooping, ankle-deep, dark
on dark, in a slow tide they might have crawled from,
scaly feet and fingers gripping rock.

But these are men, living on the hard tack
of hope, wrenching the tough salt of their wages
– a sea traffic so hidden, for all we know
scrimshaws record its tools and practices.

Methodical as potato-pickers, they bend,
sweep, gather, stow, ignoring the web
of cold that gathers between fingers and toes
and the white combs of the waves rolling up

to drown the ribbed tracks to safety. Already
men flounder in the long swell, gulping
the tide until it swallows them, mouths
open in silent Os, bodies turning

cartwheels in the undertow, pulled further
and further on the current's thread, flotsam
that drifts, tumbles, finds the shore too late –
known by a single tooth or a lucky charm.

Catching Your Breath

Kew Gardens

One February Sunday we got up early,
took the District Line to Kew, and wandered

for hours under a shared umbrella, drinking
the sappy sharpness on the edge of the year.

No one remarked us, clamped like barley sugar,
arms twisted up the umbrella stem,

filling a world under that dome with breath,
the trees around us bareskinned, indifferent.

Now it is February again, and if we still
felt shy about exposing the limbs of our love,

your wheelchair would be cover, my arms your prop.
But it is better to leave the ghosts of ourselves,

cheeks and hair damp with the rain, almost
kissing, afraid of nothing worse than Monday.

Catching Your Breath

Impressionist

In Calvin's cold city, a surprise:
gold and rose body glowing in the frame

at the top of the stairs, in the small museum.
The angle is not obvious – no pink-tipped breast,

no hand posed to tease. She turns her back, lifts
a heel – the curve of thigh, buttock, shoulder

simple and voluptuous as an apricot.
We smile, breathe her in. Later I shall think

how Impressionist is that dab of gold
on your cheek, and later still I'll wash it

carefully, day after day, capturing
the light as it dances on skin, on water

until my touch makes no more impression
than a glance brushing a woman in a frame.

Hours

Matins: I perch
on the misericord of the bed's
edge, listen for the whistle
of your lungs' chanting.

Lauds: I squat
stiff in my bones, unyielding
floor beneath me, praising
every breath you take.

Prime: I watch
the window, where grey light
is rising, salute the sound of
antiphonal blackbirds.

Terce: I bring
water for your washing
and for the sacred elements
of your medication.

Sext: I peel,
chop, simmer, stir,
enacting my faith in
the kitchen's miracles.

Nones: I read
beside you, both drowsing
through an afternoon
of blessed silence.

Vespers: I settle
your pillows, hold a straw,
kneel by the bedside
promising to stay.

Compline: I lie down
beside you, am tempted
to pray we may both wake
to a new morning.

Respite

The ambulance arrived early.
I looked at the man's clean skin, neat ears,
at a tiny mole on the woman's cheek.
Can you give me twenty minutes, I said.
No, they said, this is an emergency ambulance:
we have to be back on call in half an hour.

I wheeled you shaking from the bedroom.
It will be all right, I told you,
but they picked you up wrong,
laid you on the stretcher on your back:
you couldn't breathe.
No, you cried on a gasp.
She can't breathe on her back, I said.
They turned you on to the wrong side.
No, you cried. Stop, you cried.
She can only breathe on her left side, I said.
They took you out to the vehicle
marked Royal Berkshire Ambulance Service
in green capitals.
I couldn't reach inside to tell you
I'd be following.

I didn't know the way to the hospice:
I drove behind the ambulance, too close to the bumper,
squeezing in at roundabouts, jumping lights,
the bag like a passenger beside me with your stuff
and the two pages I'd written the night before
(when it was calm, when you were asleep):
Medication. Daily routine. How long
you'd been bedbound. What you ate.

She is highly intelligent, I'd written at the end:
she understands what is happening to her.
It is not easy for us to say goodbye.

In the room they lowered you into a bed
while I tried again to explain your one position,
the only way you could get air into your lung,
and again with your tiny pool of breath you cried
No, no, and clutched the side of the bed
until at last they found the angle

and settled you into it
and took me away
and gave me a cup of coffee in a quiet space
where I watched visitors come and go
and saw that nobody minded if they were crying.

Horace's Years

They're flying away, he says, the years, the years
and it's no use promising to live
an upright life,

keep the rules, pay your taxes, gift-aid
sums to the poor: none of this impresses
the tearless god

who's taken even the legendary heroes,
penned them in beyond that sad river
we're all going to cross –

all of us, kings or farmhands – so why
struggle to dodge war, violent storms
on the Adriatic

or the east wind sweeping across with flu
each autumn? You'll face it in the end,
that slow stream,

and the land beyond – where the wicked,
so they say, sieve water, or heave
at an endless rock.

The lease runs out on earth, on home, on love:
of all your trees it's only the dark cypress
whose shade you'll lie in

while your heir breaks into those triple-
locked cellars, crimsons the flagstones with
wine you were saving.

Rooks in February

The rookery jabbers with committees
debating sites, dimensions, settling
the status of new arrivals, authorising
repairs to wreckage of nests. Over and over
they adjourn, to soar up in a chackle
of voices, review the parishes below.

First they enact some laws for the spring:
rain to fall next Tuesday, softening the crust
of frost; daffodils after a further ten days'
extension to begin hardening, swelling
with seed; east winds to veer southwards
by the month's end.

                Now with hoarse urgency
they move the next business: judging the souls
of the recently dead. They deliberate,
pronounce. Their language is technical,
their verdicts obscure: what is the sentence
they call, call, down from the grey sky?

His Grace's Tortoise

Laud was a man of stone
(they said) – nothing beat
in that low-bred frame:
the draper's son, well-robed

peopled his solitude
with speechless companions.
Tib purred by the fire,
Hob mowed grass with his mouth.

Archiepiscopal fingers
offered fish and sallets
to rows of needle-teeth
to live-leather tongue.

Laud in the Tower
stone within stone
years on years disdained
chances of escape –

his seventy-years' head
shuddered, rolled under
the axe's crunch and tear,
steamed in the morning.

Hob in the strong shell
of himself trundled
into the next century
stringy neck stretched

under leaves, severed –
the gardener's bright edge
striking a hidden boulder
coming up bloody.

Trackside

Head's a tanned oval –
seamless rugby ball
half cradled under the shoulder
thrust upwards, bare.

A few vertebrae march
towards the sliced-off cliff
of the torso, which spills
its folded intricacies

to bulge with detail –
an anatomical section
tactlessly laid open
dark-flecked, gleaming.

On the far platform
men in yellow jackets
prepare not to flinch
from hot smells, soft

deposits on the rails,
a purpose still vibrating
along the track. We pull
away as smoothly

as if no-one's breath
had come shorter than usual
in this glass space
casual with dailiness.

Catching Your Breath

Inside the Mirror

Inside the mirror you're settled for the night,
your head tucked into the dip of the pillow,

your hands drawn up, just touching your face.
The light that's kept on for you all night, now,

falls on the curve of your shoulder, smoothing
its green cotton. I take off my shoes, lean

towards the mirror, achieve the exact angle
to hide your cannula, your oxygen tank,

the tackle of your survival. My fingers,
which are practised in touching your skin,

your sleeves – tender even towards your buttons –
undress me quickly: I don't need to break

my gaze from that framed world where your breath
comes and goes, easy, as strong as mine.

Catching Your Breath

Night Call

It's three a.m., the night service can't find us
and I've rung Kit, who can. Don't hesitate,

she told me once, nurses work odd hours:
so this odd hour – you're gasping, belly distended –

she's struggling with your catheter which still
won't draw. We wash you out again, we rock

and tilt you on the bed, pinch and elevate
the snaking plastic. At last it warms with yellow.

You pull hard on your oxygen, and grin:
Why not check the electrics while you're here?

A week ago, at full stretch on our wonky
kitchen steps, Kit fixed the ceiling light.

It shone a day or two, went bust again.
When we stop laughing, you're asleep already.

Catching Your Breath

Ruby

Crimson almost to purple – a big one, too –
the curved surface gleaming as it trembles

on the tissue you hold out to me this morning
I don't yet know is the last. Dry-mouthed

you pull on the straw we hold to your lips,
as if the smoker you once were is having

a final drag. The morning slips by, joining
one hour to the next. You take sleep's giant steps

towards the ending of what we started
another May, in a plain room that bubbled

with sunlight. The peony I cut
yesterday, to bring you the reddest thing

in the garden, is shedding its petals.
There may be as many as forty.

What the Sybil said

Easy, said the Sybil. But your going
down was hard, fighting every step
as the track narrowed. The air
was thinner each day. Colder.
Dark birds hung in the air, waiting to devour
lungs, throat.

    I let down a rope
to reach you, the rope of my arms,
of my body. I plaited into it
all my strength, knitted it with muscles
to carry slops and buckets, to bring sheets,
towels, the tilted spoonfuls of soup
at midday, sips of water in the empty
night, or in the grey seep of dawn.
It creaked with the weight of hours and minutes,
with smiles, whispered words, hands, hands.

I thought the rope might go down for ever.
I thought the rope would break.

But the last day you did not need the rope:
reaching the end of where you had to go
you laid yourself down on the lowest step.

And now, said the Sybil, looking at me,
it's your turn: *hoc labor, hic opus est.*
Climbing back. That's the hard part.

Seven Weeks

Seven weeks today. A July wind
is tousling the trees, rumpling the garden.
I have written five letters, washed the sheets.
A mistake somewhere – I've not finished
the crossword. Sit with the sounds of Sunday.
Thrashing leaves. Cows. Planes. My own breath.

All week the air has burnt: it is breath
from a lion's mouth. No stir of wind
to brush the cheeks of the sixth Sunday:
silence quivers in the house, and the garden
shrivels, as if the season's finished.
I sort bed linen. There are too many sheets.

A week leafed with letters. I scan these sheets
about you, half alert to hear your breath
until the words remind me that it's finished.
So sorry to hear. Rain in the wind
hasn't enough weight to nourish the garden.
Bells clang dryly. It is the fifth Sunday.

I wake in your presence the fourth Sunday –
not lying passive between your sheets
but laughing, striding in the summer garden
your mouth full of kisses, and your breath
sweeter and stronger than the June wind.
Why did I wake before the dream was finished?

Ready to go. *I've nothing left unfinished*
you told me once. But now beside a Sunday
river I want you here to watch the wind
curving sails, to feel the hauled sheets
as the boats put about, to taste the breath
of summer gusting down from every garden.

The second week I meet you in the garden
sitting under the oak where you once finished
fixing the swing-seat; not out of breath
but quiet and absorbed, reading the Sunday
papers, glancing up, rustling the sheets,
pinning one down that flutters in the wind.

I look out at the garden that first Sunday
when everything is finished. I smooth the sheets
and listen for your breath. There is only the wind.

Tales of the Exhumation Man:
St Pancras

Fifteen thousand to move. Long platforms,
you see. A long train. And heavy:
deep foundations. You can't just crunch through
that lot. We went in before the diggers.

A fair-sized acreage. Bear in mind
it'd been full now, a century and a half.
Bones, and the small spaces between bones.
Granddads, babies. Diphtheria. Childbirth. Pox.

No permissions, of course: no one to ask.
Whoever'd mourned them was down there too,
packed in tight, plot after plot, under
seeding grass, willowherb, the weight of soil.

Look after them, I said to my lads as we started.
Remember when we're lifting them. These are people.

Tales of the Exhumation Man:
Raising the Saint

The digging team as instructed
levered three marble fenders
with a soft explosive rip,
prised, rocked the headstone,

spade-cut with a *thunk*
through tight back-stitched grass,
shovelled, heaped, shovelled:
the pit was man-deep

when the ropes hauled and swung
the oblong box, bumping
the scraped sides, to heave
the saint into the light –

ready for the progress
towards gold and porphyry,
a niche under that dome
suspended on prayers –

and the lid creaked. Nothing.
Men rested on spade-hafts,
hands hot with the nettle-sting
memory of ropes,

pulled in mouthfuls of air
into which his molecules
had blended, an ultimate
transubstantiation.

With Gibbon in Rome

He doesn't see me, although we're here
on the same errand, fingering fluted
runnels of columns, smoothing warm
onion-skin marble.

He's dazed, this first morning, *quite incapable
of cool investigation*. The Roman sun
massages shoulders, thighs, bruised and jounced
by weeks of travelling:

This is it, he thinks, *locus iste*,
the place where since he scrawled his first declension
on the ink-stained table, he's known the grammar
holding the stones together

– and *This is it*, I think: *perpetual, inscription* –
the root of our big words. But it's wilder
than we expected: green tongues of weeds
thrust from a curved wall

marking Vesta's temple; swallows swing
through the indiscriminate blue that pours
round pillars, basilicas, jumbled heaps
where a blackbird fossicks.

Leaning against the Arch of Titus
beside me, he peoples the cracked pavements
with consuls, senators, the divine Augustus,
watches the empire grow,

decay, immortal Latin invade the provinces,
till as the sun slips behind the Palatine,
and the chant swells from the grey church,
its cadences periodic

as Cicero (*here, where Tully spoke*)
an edifice of his own begins to rise
from the ancient marsh, stone on stone –
here, where Caesar fell.

Catching Your Breath

Turn

Hermes is my dream-god, joining the hands
of Eurydice and Orpheus, in the iron twilight

where for a moment they're allowed to gaze,
drink each other in. The god inclines his head

with a half-smile, watching. The bargain has been made
which Orpheus will break: he starts to trek

up towards light, to listen, to wonder why
no breath is following him. How should she breathe,

all air as she is? but he falters and turns
just as I turn, in the dreams the god sends me

where you may be dancing, standing in the garden,
lying in my arms – till I break some rule

and Hermes looks at me, knowing I shall wake
to find you dissolving, a shadow on the wind.

Catching Your Breath

Feather

On the lawn, a scrap of silk, no wider
than a double grass-blade, drops of cream

patterning the brown. Rub it, and the filaments
split, tangle: fingers can't re-align them

as a beak once did. Was this fabric
knitted into a wing? What gloss, what loss

does it record? Did some Cathy Earnshaw,
tugging handfuls of feathers from her pillows,

long to burst out of the walls of her body,
soar with this into the wild air?

I keep it for a day or two, as if
to bring you a small find from the garden

you've not seen, as if we'll laugh together
at my childishness. Then let the wind take it.

Catching Your Breath

Absolute

Looking at this shot I took, just hours
after you'd died, on the film that got stuck

in the camera, as if it knew how much
I did and didn't want to have it printed

till now, two years later – without any attempt
to get it out until yesterday in the shop

when the girl inserted the camera and both
hands inside a black box to manipulate

through integral gloves as if she were barrier nursing
– I feel a thud of shock at what I'd forgotten,

how your face had shrunk, how a rim of bone
thrust at the skin above your closed eyes,

and on sheets that seemed, if anything, less lifeless
than this mask, how absolute was your absence.

Horace in Mourning

Why should we be quiet or restrained
about your death? It's lamentation
we need now, the cries of the tragic muse.

That sleep you longed for has you in its grip,
and already we're missing your sharp eye
for injustice, your integrity.

So many, my love, to mourn for you!
– but even the bitter gift of the poet
can't sing you back from death:

not even Orpheus (who, the story goes,
magicked trees into listening)
could make the blood flow in your veins

or re-open that gate you've passed through.
Hard stuff. And all we've got is patience
reminding us that nothing can be changed.

Pruning, with Chaffinches

Mid-February, still dormant. Grass bleached by winter
but the sap will be rising soon. Yesterday
a solo chaffinch, staccato, hesitant –

today, as I fetch secateurs, loppers, saw,
rivals are bowling each other out, exhaustless,
fluent. The trick in pruning is to square

art with mechanics – check for disease, the cross
and rub of branches, then aim to let light
into the centre. I set the open jaws

wide, squeeze: a solid *clop*, and the cut
length poises among the tangle, sways,
rattles down. The tree hooks off my hat,

combs my hair with a twig. I step back, scrutinise,
pace like an oil painter. Was it Reynolds said
he walked miles in his studio, eyeing the canvas?

Clop, clop. Twenty years ago we planted
together, choosing this gap in the dormant time
to stake and firm a stick-thin stem, broad

now as my body, limbs thicker than mine.
I haul into the tree, uneasy tomboy,
brace muscles, slither and rock, regain

balance. The blade grates. Thin snow
of sawdust powders the ground. A branch falls.
Between the chaffinch calls I half-hear you

warning me to be careful with edge-tools.

Reading Horace in the Third Millennium

Your woods creak under snow, groan and crack
through gales; your vines are pruned to shape,
fields ploughed; in storms the middle sea

clashes its teeth against the coast, black
depths rolling with power: all these
weathers endure. Trickier to handle

are the wine-jars whose fragments
tease archaeologists – far from the rub
of daily hands on their round bellies,

the heft and tilt and hiccupping glug
of pouring. Odder still, the hair
oozing, trickling with oil, scratchy

with myrtle twigs the revellers have twisted –
heedless of ants – before they leap and dance
to honour the ambiguous gods. Footnotes

plod on the track of names – the patrons, friends,
generals, politicians, neighbours
whose network encircles that Sabine farm

where you entertained, and walked, and wrote
at the centre of the world, certain of nothing
but what needs no explanation: that love

burns, delights and teases; that a feast
binds friends together; and that death
knocks on every door. On every door.

With Vincent in the South

Astounded by the light
I take
your picture from the pocket of my heart
to warm it in this place
we didn't see together
imagining that you can feel the sun

here where he saw the sky
swirl
corn glitter
stones vibrate

pounded by radiance

he ladled paint
thick as eggs in cream

the landscape empty now
of popes and painters
gives its impartial blessing
washes eyes with light

grief too
finds asylum here
sheds some of its weight

Walk

for my sister

Afternoon sun on the via Appia
a trigonometry of light: angled pines,
shadows striping the road in parallels,
the long vista southwards

paved by rounded stones, shiny
with feet and centuries, loaf-tops,
bun-tops, their fit at best
approximate:

we slither, flat-level mountaineering
past breaches pooled with brown water,
cracks one could twist an ankle in
– down one, a perfect cone

potent with seeds to push
another pine tree up, or twenty
while high and invisible a serin
rasps out its song,

a black redstart on a tomb
flicks, eyes us, flirts away
into the miles of haze, of scent,
of quiet

till no-one's left on the road with us
but Cicero's ghost tramping into exile
as Caesar leaves the city another way
to march to Gaul.

Caliban

I stood on the shore for a long time, watching
that amazing tree of wings belly out,
begin to sway, surge, swim with the tide,
grow smaller, until the line on the edge
of seeing wavered and everything
was still again. The sea licked, licked.

The island rang with bird cries, and the slow
pulse of the waves. I lay down on the headland,
pressed my length into the turf, listened
to the tide humming along my blood, then
rolled over and looked at the sky. No one
measured my doing, my being. The air
was empty.

Cockles, limpets, berries. It is a feast.
Walnuts. The heath at the top of the island. Springs
and freshets. The long views, secret hideouts
in bracken or under the lip of a cave. Trees.

Tomorrow is another feast of waking,
tramping the wild circle of rocks. I can run,
can dawdle: time to smell every clump
of weed. The fish will wait for me. The sun
will be slow going down.

I begin to stretch my legs.

Notes

Horace in Winter

This and the other Horace poems are versions or responses rather than strict translations. These three come from, respectively, *Odes* Book One, 9; 4; Book Three, 30.

On the Beach at Aldeburgh

This tribute to the late Julia Casterton is partly influenced by her poem 'My Second Resurrection' in *The Doves of Finisterre.*

Horace at Sea

A version of *Odes* Book One, 5.

Fitzroy

The shipping area Finisterre was renamed Fitzroy a few years ago. In her novel *Monkey Business*, Jenny Diski presents Fitzroy's suicide as partly the result of his contact with the 'free-thinking' Darwin, years earlier.

Horace's Years

A version of *Odes* Book Two, 14.

What the Sybil said

Easy: the words of the Sybil to Aeneas as he prepares to go down to the Underworld: 'It's easy to go down to Hell, but coming back is hard.'

With Gibbon in Rome

In his *Memoir*, when describing the impetus for *Decline and Fall*, Gibbon writes that he was so overwhelmed by his first few days in Rome as to be 'quite incapable of cool investigation'.

Horace in Mourning

An adaptation of *Odes* Book One, 24.

Pruning, with Chaffinches

The rapid call of the chaffinch has been compared to a cricketer running up to bowl.